6—
Scan

Churchill
on
COURAGE

Churchill on COURAGE

TIMELESS WISDOM
FOR PERSEVERING

Frederick Talbott

A JANET THOMA BOOK

THOMAS NELSON PUBLISHERS
Nashville • Atlanta • London • Vancouver

Published in Nashville, Tennessee, by Thomas Nelson, Inc., Publishers, and distributed in Canada by Word Communications, Ltd., Richmond, British Columbia.

Library of Congress Cataloging-in-Publication Data

Talbott, Frederick.
    Churchill on courage : timeless wisdom for persevering / Frederick Talbott.
       p.   cm.
    ISBN 0-7852-7410-3 (hc)
    1. Churchill, Winston, Sir, 1874–1965—Quotations. 2. Courage—Quotations, maxims, etc. 3. Quotations, English. I. Title.
DA566.9.C5T25 1996
941.084′092—dc20
                                             96–27956
                                              CIP

Printed in the United States of America
1 2 3 4 5 6 — 01 00 99 98 97 96

To my mother and father
for sharing the lessons of
courage and goodness,
and to all who live by and share
these essential values.

Acknowledgments

I give thanks to Sir Winston Churchill. Many inspire nations; Churchill inspired a century. I believe he will continue to share the gift of courage for many centuries to come.

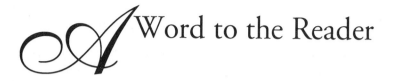Word to the Reader

Courage is essential to leadership. It is the fundamental process that moves the vision of leadership from idea to action.

I began focusing on courage after completing *Shakespeare on Leadership* in 1994. It was then that I recognized the life and voice and calling of Sir Winston Churchill.

Nothing seemed to come easy to Winston Churchill. He was not a gifted student—he was placed at the lowest level of learners at his school. Nor was he athletically gifted. And, by his own account, he was terrified to the point of illness before sharing his first public speech. Yet here was the man who went on to become a master horseman and cavalry officer, to win the Nobel Prize for Literature, to lead Great Britain through the abyss of World War II and economic reconstruction, and to be hailed as the greatest orator of the century.

Churchill knew courage as a constant, irrepressible call to duty, despite hardship, rejection, and failure. His was the lone voice calling for war preparation amid a national policy of appeasement to Nazi Germany. His was the remarkable voice, at the age of sixty-five, that rallied a nation and the free world to overcome and defeat the Axis terror. And the voice that, after defeat, returned to office in his seventy-fifth year to guide Britain through economic and Cold War crises.

In all my reading of Churchill's works I have discovered two keys that lend valuable insight. The first was his absolute, unshakable dedication to duty and his determination to take a stand for what he believed to be right. The second was his belief in sharing courage with others. Indeed, this master of the English language appeared to most favor the word *we*.

I have focused on Churchill's speeches because they best share his voice, the voice of courage. Selections are arranged chronologically to reflect the breadth of his message. I have added brief interpretation and historical perspective. I encourage you to apply each passage to your life and add your own essential perspective.

This book is written for everyone, for all of us must muster the courage to meet life's challenges and make our way.

In *Great Contemporaries*, Churchill wrote, "Courage is rightly esteemed the first of human qualities, because, as has been said, it is the quality which guarantees all others." Courage is a commitment of the spirit essential to challenge doubt, impose will, protect integrity, prevent harm, initiate action, advance values, and break the chains of fear and hardship. Courage, when spurred by a belief in goodness, is essential to all progress. Recognize, by considering the words that follow, that one person's courage can make a remarkable and lasting difference.

*C*onsider your principles, consider your cause.

Announcing candidacy, Manchester, April 29, 1904

In this election address, Churchill urged followers to match actions and beliefs, calling for an economy favoring justice and "human liberty."

*N*ow you know where we stand.

Dundee, May 1, 1908

In yet another election address, he asked voters
to focus on his record and values,
not simply campaign rhetoric.

Churchill ON COURAGE

*W*e are always changing, like nature we change a great deal, although we change always very slowly. We always change, and consequently we are always reaching a higher level after each change, but yet with the harmony of our life unbroken and unimpaired.

Dundee, May 4, 1908

Voters were encouraged to appreciate the contributions of all classes and people, as all were essential to the eternal advancement of liberty.

Churchill ON COURAGE

*L*et us build wisely, let us build surely, let us build faithfully, let us build not for the moment, but for the years that are to come, and so establish here below what we hope to find above—a house of many mansions, where there shall be room for all.

Dundee, May 4, 1908

Churchill believed all have a duty to build for the advancement of all.

Churchill ON COURAGE

$\mathcal{P}$romises are the blowing
of glittering bubbles;
performances are the molding
and hammering of iron.

Dundee, May 7, 1908

In this election address, Churchill declared that trust
should be based on achievement, not mere promises.

Churchill ON COURAGE

I have a high and
prevailing faith in the
essential goodness of great
peoples.

Swansea, August 14, 1908

Churchill fostered faith in the good of others.

Churchill ON COURAGE

*W*hat is the use of living if it be not to strive for noble causes and to make this muddled world a better place for those who will live in it after we are gone?

Dundee, October 9, 1908

His address to the Scottish Liberal Association asked for continued support for his Liberal Party and policies designed to advance society.

Churchill ON COURAGE

*W*e are going—swinging bravely forward along the grand high road—and already behind the distant mountains is the promise of the sun.

Dundee, October 9, 1908

From his earliest political involvement, Churchill shared a special, hope-filled vision of the future. He urged all to venture courageously.

*H*umanity will not be cast down.

Dundee, October 8, 1908

He urged all to be steadfast, enduring, and invincible while facing considerable social and labor challenges.

Churchill ON COURAGE

A great battle lies before us, but united, concentrated, combined, working together in true comradeship, there is no foe who can bar our path.

Dundee, January 18, 1910

Despite a disappointing election, Churchill called for a united, determined, and invincible leadership team.

We shall proceed through our course with firmness and patience.

Dundee, September 11, 1912

Amid bitter political fighting, he called for his constituents to avoid the overreaction expressed by their opponents.

Churchill ON COURAGE

*T*he nose of the bulldog
has been slanted
backwards so that he can breathe
without letting go.

Description of Naval strategy, 1914

As First Lord of the Admiralty, Churchill called
for naval expansion and strengthening to create a
sufficient and lasting defense for the island nation.

Churchill ON COURAGE

*L*ook forward, do not look backward. Gather afresh in heart and spirit all the energies of your being, bend anew together for a supreme effort.

War report, Dundee, June 5, 1915

Amid the threat of demotion from his Admiralty role and the threats and disappointments of war, Churchill called for all to dedicate their energies to present and future challenges.

Churchill ON COURAGE

*W*e are passing through a bad time now, and it will probably be worse before it is better, but that it will be better, if we only endure and persevere, I have no doubt whatever.

House of Commons, November 15, 1915

Churchill's gravest error was his support for the invasion of the Dardanelles, resulting in thousands of British casualties. The resulting scandal forced his resignation from his post as Lord of Admiralty, and many predicted the end of his public service. Despite this, he shared a vision of a challenging and better future.

Churchill ON COURAGE

*T*he truth is incontrovertible. Panic may resent it, ignorance may deride it, malice may distort it, but there it is.

House of Commons, May 17, 1916

Churchill, a master debater, insisted that truth stands every measure.

Churchill ON COURAGE

$\mathcal{Y}$ou must look boldly for new fields and new methods of manoeuvre.

Army estimates, House of Commons, March 5, 1917

Churchill urged the House to avoid reluctance and advance its war efforts.

Churchill ON COURAGE

Our dangers are great, but our opportunity is incomparable.

Dundee, July 21, 1917

As newly appointed Minister of Munitions, he encouraged Britain to stand as "a rock" while awaiting the United States' intervention in the Great War.

Churchill ON COURAGE

*V*ictory is not a vague or intangible thing. It is represented by solid facts.

Middlesex, October 9, 1917

In this speech, stressing his belief that true victory is braced in certainty, Churchill elevated the spirit of munitions workers.

Churchill ON COURAGE

*T*he greatest storm of all is gathering, the thunderclouds are banking up, minute after minute, before our eyes. Have good confidence. Let us not for one moment lose our unshakable confidence that right will triumph.

London, January 11, 1918

Churchill here urged the United States to join the war effort to establish victory and peace, and share its faith in the power of goodness.

Churchill ON COURAGE

*T*he greatest actions of men or nations are spontaneous and instinctive. They do not result from nice calculations or long processes of thought. They happen as if nothing could help them happening. The heart, as the French say, has reasons which the reason does not know.

Westminster, July 4, 1918

After almost four years of war, Churchill urged the Liberty Day crowd to recognize the essential call of freedom.

Churchill ON COURAGE

Our intentions are just. They are not dictated by vengeance or hatred.

War effort, Sheffield, October 11, 1918

Churchill reminded his audience to remember that the future of Britain was the true issue of the war.

There can only be one maxim: Full steam ahead.

War effort, Manchester, October 15, 1918

Amid armistice negotiations, he urged Britain on to full victory and a just and lasting peace.

*I*t is very important not to underrate the problem. It is also very important not to overrate it.

London, November 7, 1918

Armistice terms were presented to Germany, fighting continued, and Churchill looked ahead to the challenges of demobilization while urging his countrymen to face problems squarely.

Churchill ON COURAGE

*W*e are not through the
winter of our task yet.
There will possibly be a period of
hard weather. But the spring is
coming, and we look forward
to a brilliant and glorious
summertime.

Middlesex, January 2, 1919

Despite post-war hardships, Churchill spoke of a
hope-filled future.

Churchill ON COURAGE

*T*he more we succeed in eliminating selfish interests, which are not proportioned to the guidance, exertion, and skill contributed, the more solid will be the foundations on which we build, and the greater and the more abundant will be our reward.

Middlesex, January 2, 1919

Churchill saw an immediate need to eliminate the imbalances of selfishness, calling for all to contribute unselfishly to avoid social poverty.

Churchill ON COURAGE

To win . . . there must be absolute faithfulness on all sides.

Middlesex, January 2, 1919

The nation, he insisted, must unite in both resolve and duty to ensure prosperity and the conquest of post-war challenges.

Churchill ON COURAGE

We can do it if we try.

Middlesex, January 2, 1919

Churchill shared enduring faith in his fellow citizens, including all in this call for unity and determination.

Churchill ON COURAGE

*T*here are two maxims which should always be acted upon in the hour of victory: Do not be carried away by success into demanding or taking more than is right or prudent. Do not disband your army until you have got your terms.

House of Commons, March 3, 1919

Demobilization, the occupation of Germany, and armament questions prompted Churchill to remind all to be just, forever prepared and vigilant to avoid anarchy.

*W*e have got to stand together.

London, March 13, 1919

Churchill declared that unity is essential to face pressing domestic and international challenges.

We are weakened and we are tired, but we are not done yet.

London, February 17, 1920

Amid a world torn by turmoil and confusion, he urged perseverance and faith.

Churchill ON COURAGE

We are evidently in for a hard fight.

Leicester, November 30, 1923

The rigors of a sudden election prompted Churchill to acknowledge the challenge of mounting political conflict.

Churchill ON COURAGE

The first duty of a warship is to keep afloat.

House of Commons, March 7, 1930

He called for the construction and continued service of heavily armored battleships amid pressure for disarmament, insisting that they were essential to the nation's survival.

Churchill ON COURAGE

*T*he progress of the world is dependent on eminent individuals. It has never been ground out by political machines.

New York City, January 25, 1932

During this press interview, he shared his belief that individuals, not politics, best advance great causes and nations.

Churchill ON COURAGE

$\mathcal{W}$ars come very suddenly.

House of Commons, February 7, 1934

Churchill warned that Britain must have the might
to back up its armament limits of Germany and
avoid harm.

Churchill ON COURAGE

We must be independent. We must be free.

House of Commons, March 8, 1934

Amid cries for appeasement and reliance on allies, Churchill called for Britain to establish military might and independence.

Churchill ON COURAGE

*I*f we prepare, our preparation should not be too late.

London Broadcast, November 16, 1934

Churchill warned that plans must be timely to be effective. He called for "statesmanship, expense, and exertion," including the immediate development of the greatest air power in Europe.

Churchill ON COURAGE

$\mathcal{P}$ending some new discovery, the only direct measure of defence upon a great scale is the certainty of being able to inflict simultaneously upon the enemy as great damage as he can inflict upon ourselves.

House of Commons, November 28, 1934

Citing the need to match and exceed opposing strength, Churchill urged British production of warplanes to meet the Nazi air threat—and possibly prevent war.

Churchill ON COURAGE

*I*t is always a great
mistake to put people in
a position where human nature
may be too highly tried.

House of Commons, July 12, 1935

Churchill warned the House about conveying too
much trust and power to future ministers.

Churchill ON COURAGE

We know where we are and what we are going to do, and we also know what we are not going to do.

Chingford, October 8, 1935

Following Italy's invasion of Abyssinia, Churchill urged immediate armament and support of the League of Nations' sanctions against aggression.

Churchill ON COURAGE

$\mathcal{S}$ome responsibility rests upon the conduct of our own affairs.

House speech, March 26, 1936

After the German conquest of the Rhineland, Churchill pledged confidence that the British government would best prepare to meet the coming threat.

Churchill ON COURAGE

*N*o one is compelled to serve great causes unless he feels fit for it, but nothing is more certain than that you cannot take the lead in great causes as a half-timer.

Chingford, May 8, 1936

Following Italy's triumph over Abyssinia, Churchill called for Britain's full support of the League of Nations.

Churchill ON COURAGE

We must recognise that we have a great treasure to guard; that the inheritance in our possession represents the prolonged achievement of the centuries; that there is not one of our simple uncounted rights today for which better men than we are have not died on the scaffold or the battlefield. We have not only a great treasure; we have a great cause. Are we taking every measure within our power to defend that cause?

Paris, September 24, 1936

Churchill saw the world divided into nations led by Nazis, nations led by Bolshevists, and a free world of nations led by their own people. He urged those committed to individual liberty to honor and defend their cause.

Churchill ON COURAGE

*I*f things were going very badly, how glad one would be to see him come 'round the corner.

Memorial to Lawrence of Arabia, Oxford High School, October 3, 1936

Churchill's praise of T.E. Lawrence, famous for his bold leadership during the Arab revolt of 1916-18, summoned the image of courage.

Churchill ON COURAGE

He was indeed a dweller upon the mountaintops where the air is cold, crisp, and rarefied, and where the view on clear days commands all the kingdoms of the world and the glory of them.

Memorial to Lawrence of Arabia, Oxford High School, October 3, 1936

In honoring Lawrence the hero, Churchill shared the vision of the mighty.

Churchill ON COURAGE

I recall the story of Lord St. Vincent, who, in his anxiety at the cutting down of oak trees required for the ships of the navy, planted an acorn wherever he went. Those who do not think of the future are unworthy of their ancestors.

Tribute to the Royal Marines, London, October 24, 1936

Churchill shared a heartfelt tribute to all who build for and honor the future.

*T*here is a profound and almost universal conviction throughout the land that we shall not escape our dangers by recoiling from them. The time has come when we must confront them and surmount them.

City Carlton Club, London, June 28, 1939

He insisted that Nazi aggression must be met, and feelings of uncertainty must be replaced with absolute commitment.

Churchill ON COURAGE

Carry on, and dread nought.

House of Commons, December 6, 1939

Responding to the raging war at sea, Churchill called for all to project their courage, abandon fear, and do their utmost duty.

Churchill ON COURAGE

*T*his is no time for ease and comfort. It is the time to dare and endure.

Manchester, January 27, 1940

He cited the urgent need to ration the nation's resources to best prepare "for the task we have at hand."

Churchill ON COURAGE

*C*riticism in the body politic is like pain in the human body. It is not pleasant, but where would the body be without it? No health or sensibility would be possible without continued correctives and warnings of pain.

Free Trade Hall, Manchester, January 27, 1940

Churchill predicted that the Nazi practice of silencing all critics would lead to Germany's downfall.

*C*ome then: let us to the task, to the battle, to the toil—each to our part, each to our station.

Free Trade Hall, Manchester, January 27, 1940

After five months of war, Churchill urged his people to make every essential commitment to build a great army to overcome the might of the enemy.

*T*here is not a week, nor a day, nor an hour to lose.

Free Trade Hall, Manchester, January 27, 1940

He insisted that time was of the essence when preparing for the mounting conflict.

Churchill ON COURAGE

$\mathcal{C}$ome then, let us go forward together with our united strength.

House of Commons, May 13, 1940

At age sixty-five, Churchill saw his new roles as Prime Minister and Minister of Defense as opportunities to inspire the respect and support of his fellows. With this speech he sparked the courage of a nation.

Churchill ON COURAGE

*Y*ou ask: "What is our aim?" I can answer in one word: It is victory, victory at all costs, victory in spite of all terror, victory, however long and hard the road may be; for without victory there is no survival.

House of Commons, May 13, 1940

The newly appointed Prime Minister shared his belief that victory in war is essential to national survival.

Churchill ON COURAGE

I have nothing to offer but blood, toil, tears, and sweat.

House of Commons, May 13, 1940

This speech, summoning a national commitment to courageous leadership, marked the turning point from the hesitance of the Chamberlain government. Britain was now led by a lion.

Our task is not only to win the battle—but to win the war.

London Broadcast, May 19, 1940

Germany had broken through French defensive positions, unleashing its blitzkrieg on the nation across the English Channel. Churchill saw the coming storm.

*N*ever to surrender
ourselves to servitude
and shame, whatever the cost and
the agony may be.

London Broadcast, May 19, 1940

Holland had fallen, France was under siege, and
Britain was clearly in the path of Hitler's frenzy.
Churchill knew the absolute necessity to motivate
every British citizen to the challenge.

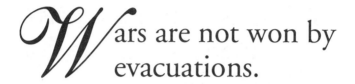

*W*ars are not won by evacuations.

House of Commons, June 4, 1940

More than 300,000 British and French troops had been rescued from the French beach head and transported to England. Amid celebration of the effort, Churchill redirected his countrymen to the immediate need to fully commit to the fight for victory.

Churchill ON COURAGE

I think that no idea is so outlandish that it should not be considered with a searching but at the same time with a steady eye.

House of Commons, June 4, 1940

Citing the wicked inventiveness of the coming foe, Churchill hailed the creative spirit of Britain as a vital resource to thwart invasion.

Churchill ON COURAGE

*W*e shall not flag or fail. We shall go on to the end. We shall fight in France, we shall fight on the seas and oceans, we shall fight with growing confidence and growing strength in the air. We shall defend our island, whatever the cost may be. We shall fight on the beaches, we shall fight on the landing grounds, we shall fight in the fields and in the streets, we shall fight in the hills. We shall never surrender.

House of Commons, June 4, 1940

This speech, in the darkest days of war, sounded the eternal call of courage.

Churchill ON COURAGE

*I*f we can stand up to him, all Europe may be free and the life of the world may move forward into broad, sunlit uplands. But if we fail, then the whole world, including the United States, including all that we have known and cared for, will sink into the abyss of a new Dark Age made more sinister, and perhaps more protracted, by the light of perverted science. Let us therefore brace ourselves to our duties, and so bear ourselves that, if the British Empire and its Commonwealth last for a thousand years, men will say: "This was their finest hour."

House of Commons, June 18, 1940

One of Churchill's most famous speeches underscores the majesty of collective courage. The Battle of France was over, and now Churchill expected the full fury of Germany to be directed at his island. The stage was set for the Battle of Britain.

Churchill ON COURAGE

*H*ere in this strong city of refuge which enshrines the title deeds of human progress and is of deep consequence to Christian civilization. . . . We await undismayed the impending assault. Perhaps it will come tonight. Perhaps it will come next week. Perhaps it will never come. We must show ourselves equally capable of meeting a sudden violent shock or—what is perhaps a harder test—a prolonged vigil. But be the ordeal sharp, or long, or both, we shall seek no terms, we shall tolerate no parley; we may show mercy—we shall ask for none.

London Broadcast, July 14, 1940

The first stage of Operation Sea Lion—the German code name for the invasion of Britain—began with air attacks designed to destroy the Royal Air Force. The Battle of Britain was now underway. Prime Minister Churchill called for all to persevere with diligence and absolute resolve.

Churchill ON COURAGE

*T*he road to victory may not be so long as we expect. But we have no right to count upon this. Be it long or short, rough or smooth, we mean to reach our journey's end.

House of Commons, August 20, 1940

He reminded all of the united and absolute effort to defend Britain.

Churchill ON COURAGE

*N*ever in the field of human conflict was so much owed by so many to so few.

House of Commons, August 20, 1940

Churchill's praise of the Royal Air Force victory over the Luftwaffe reminds us to always honor our champions.

Churchill ON COURAGE

This is a time for everyone to stand together and hold firm, as they are doing.

London Broadcast, September 11, 1940

Churchill manifested collective courage to overcome the terror of the night bombing of London.

Churchill ON COURAGE

We shall rather draw from the heart of suffering itself the means of inspiration and survival.

London Broadcast, September 11, 1940

Churchill praised Londoners' courage and fortitude during attack, adding that their valiant stand sends courage and belief to British troops everywhere.

Churchill ON COURAGE

I am confident that we shall succeed in defeating and largely destroying this most tremendous onslaught by which we are now threatened, and anyhow, whatever happens, we will all go down fighting to the end. I feel as sure as the sun will rise tomorrow that we shall be victorious.

House of Commons, September 17, 1940

With the detection of a massive German sea transport system, Churchill forecasted the imminent invasion of Britain and the need to be ready to repel it.

Churchill ON COURAGE

*D*eath and sorrow will be the companions of our journey; hardship our garment; constancy and valor our only shield. We must be united, we must be undaunted, we must be inflexible.

House of Commons, October 8, 1940

Churchill predicted "long, dark months" of war and calamity, yet insisted that courage and unity would stand the test.

Churchill ON COURAGE

*W*hen good people get into trouble because they are attacked and heavily smitten by the vile and wicked, they must be very careful not to get at loggerheads with one another.

Broadcast to France, October 21, 1940

Churchill advised the conquered French to unite for freedom and recognize the disruptive intent of the enemy.

Churchill ON COURAGE

*W*e just must make the best of things as they come along.

Broadcast to France, October 21, 1940

The British Prime Minister urged the French to join the British in transforming problems into opportunities for victory.

Churchill ON COURAGE

*G*ood night, then: sleep to gather strength for the morning. For the morning will come. Brightly it will shine on the brave and true, kindly upon all who suffer for the cause, glorious upon the tombs of heroes. Thus will shine the dawn.

Broadcast to France, October 21, 1940

Churchill masterfully shared the metaphor of dawn to promote hope.

Churchill ON COURAGE

*T*he watchword we must carry must be that vigilance must be unceasing.

House of Commons, December 19, 1940

Victories in the field revealed the might and readiness of the British forces.

Churchill ON COURAGE

Criticism is easy; achievement is more difficult.

House of Commons, January 22, 1941

At sixty-six, Churchill reminded those critical of the war effort to recognize the immediate and pressing challenges at hand.

Churchill ON COURAGE

*W*e shall not fail or falter; we shall not weaken or tire. Neither the sudden shock of battle nor the long-drawn trials of vigilance and exertion will wear us down. Give us the tools, and we will finish the job.

London Broadcast, February 9, 1941

Churchill was greatly impressed by President Roosevelt's encouraging letter citing Longfellow's "Sail on, O Ship of State!" He urged the American president to "put your faith in us," while calling for Britain to prepare, equip, and endure to victory.

Churchill ON COURAGE

The fortunes of war are fickle and changing. But an act of shame would deprive us of the respect which we now enjoy throughout the world, and this would sap the vitals of our strength.

Broadcast, London, April 27, 1941

Greece and Yugoslavia had fallen to Germany, London was under air siege, and the war at sea was taking its toll. At this dire and uncertain time, Churchill proclaimed, "Our policy and conduct should be upon the highest level, and that honour should be our guide."

Churchill ON COURAGE

The only answer to defeat is victory.

House speech, June 10, 1941

The German battleship Bismarck was destroyed, but major challenges remained on all fronts. Churchill insisted that victory as an absolute standard be the essential message of British leadership during the war.

Churchill ON COURAGE

*L*ift up your hearts. All will come right. Out of the depths of sorrow and sacrifice will be born again the glory of mankind.

London, June 12, 1941

Churchill repeatedly sounded the call of eternal faith and hope amid the hell storm of the German blitzkrieg.

Churchill ON COURAGE

Our solid, stubborn strength has stood the awful test.

London, June 12, 1941

The Prime Minister hailed the collective resilience of the British people during the twenty-second month of war.

Churchill ON COURAGE

With the help of God, of which we must all feel daily conscious, we shall continue steadfast in faith and duty till our task is done.

London, June 12, 1941

Churchill pledged utmost faith in divine guidance as the nation prepared to resist imminent invasion.

*S*trong tides of emotion, fierce surges of passion, sweep the broad expanses of the Union in this year of fate. In that prodigious travail there are many elemental forces, there is much heart-searching and self-questioning; some pangs, some sorrow, some conflict of voices, but no fear.

Broadcast to the U.S., June 16, 1941

Churchill's remarkable broadcast to the United States assured all listeners that Britain—fueled by the two nations' collective spirit—would be victorious.

Churchill ON COURAGE

When great causes are on the move in the world, stirring all men's souls, drawing them from their firesides, casting aside comfort, wealth, and the pursuit of happiness in response to impulses at once awestriking and irresistible, we learn that we are spirits, not animals, and that something is going on in space and time and beyond space and time, which, whether we like it or not, spells duty.

Broadcast to the U.S., June 16, 1941

The British leader urged those in the United States to heed the call of great causes.

*N*ot so easily shall the lights of freedom die.

Broadcast to the U.S., June 16, 1941

He shared the view that the United States was needed to play a pivotal role in the preservation of freedom.

Churchill ON COURAGE

United, we can save and guide the world.

Broadcast to the U.S., June 16, 1941

Churchill urged Americans to recognize that world salvation is a fundamental duty.

*U*pon that rock, all stood unshakable.

London, July 14, 1941

Churchill praised the extraordinary courage and perseverance of the British amid the ongoing German attack and resulting hardships.

*N*othing is more dangerous in wartime than to live in the temperamental atmosphere of a Gallup poll, always feeling one's pulse and taking one's temperature. I see it said that leaders should keep their ears to the ground. All I can say is that the British nation will find it very hard to look up to the leaders who are detected in that somewhat ungainly posture.

House of Commons, September 30, 1941

Churchill urged his critics to heed the call of their wisdom and values, recognizing mass opinion, no matter how well intended, may at times be misinformed.

*N*ever give in, never give in, never, never, never, never—in nothing great or small, large or petty—never give in except to convictions of honor and good sense.

Harrow School, October 29, 1941

Churchill, honored by a new verse in the song of his alma mater, called on all to never yield their values.

*D*o not let us speak of darker days; let us speak rather of sterner days. These are not dark days: these are great days—the greatest days our country has ever lived; and we must all thank God that we have been allowed, each of us according to our stations, to play a part in making these days memorable in the history of our race.

Harrow School, October 29, 1941

He urged all present at Harrow to view the challenge all the British faced as an historic opportunity.

Churchill ON COURAGE

*W*e kept on doing our best, we kept on improving. We profited by our mistakes and our experiences. We turned misfortune to good account.

Hull, November 7, 1941

Hull had been devastated by enemy bombing. Churchill reminded its citizens that each test, each hurt, and each hardship shares valuable insight—which leads to renewed confidence and strength.

Churchill ON COURAGE

*H*owever hard the task may be, I know you will all be ready for that high moment.

Sheffield, November 8, 1941

Sheffield, too, had endured the Nazi bombing. Churchill let all present know the nation was inspired by their confidence and determination.

Churchill ON COURAGE

*W*e have not journeyed all this way across the centuries, across the oceans, across the mountains, across the prairies, because we are made of sugar candy.

Canadian Senate and House of Commons, Ottawa, December 30, 1941

This speech and broadcast, citing the collective heritage of courage, is often hailed as Churchill's finest at a pivotal point in the war. Japan had attacked Pearl Harbor, the U.S. had entered the war, and Churchill's confidence was unshakable.

Churchill ON COURAGE

*I*f anybody likes to play rough, we can play rough too.

Ottawa, Canada, December 30, 1941

Churchill promised to answer enemy challenges with ferocity.

*N*either the length of the
struggle nor any form
of severity which it may assume
shall make us weary or shall make
us quit.

Ottawa, Canada, December 30, 1941

He then pledged absolute dedication to victory.

Churchill ON COURAGE

_T_here shall be no halting or half measures, there shall be no compromise or parley.

Ottawa, Canada, December 30, 1941

Focusing on British resolve, Churchill spoke of full and complete dedication to the war effort.

Churchill ON COURAGE

*T*he crisis is upon us. . . .
We cannot for a
moment afford to relax. On the
contrary, we must drive ourselves
forward with unrelenting zeal.

Ottawa, Canada, December 30, 1941

Amid the exhaustive pressures of the German
assault, the British Prime Minister encouraged all
to make unrelenting strides to defend the island and
defeat Germany.

Churchill ON COURAGE

*T*here is no room now for the dilettante, the weakling, for the shirker, or the sluggard.

Ottawa, Canada, December 30, 1941

Strength, Churchill insisted, must be complete and universal.

Churchill ON COURAGE

*T*he enemies ranged against us, coalesced and combined against us, have asked for total war. Let us make sure they get it.

Ottawa, Canada, December 30, 1941

This public declaration of absolute, total war sent a firm message to the German high command.

Churchill ON COURAGE

$\mathcal{S}$ome chicken! Some neck!

Ottawa, Canada, December 30, 1941

Churchill celebrated the victory of the British in preventing the German invasion by citing a prediction by French generals a year earlier: "In three weeks England will have her neck wrung like a chicken" by Nazi Germany. Churchill's response is cited above.

We have suffered together and we shall conquer together.

Ottawa, Canada, December 30, 1941

He reminded the Canadian people of collective suffering and future, united conquest of the enemy.

Churchill ON COURAGE

So far we have not failed. We shall not fail now.

London Broadcast, February 15, 1942

The British surrender in Singapore prompted public fear and doubt, which Churchill countered with this pledge.

Churchill ON COURAGE

*H*owever tempting it might be to some when much trouble lies ahead to step aside adroitly and put someone else up to take the blows, the heavy and repeated blows, which are coming, I do not intend to adopt that cowardly course, but, on the contrary, to stand to my post and persevere in accordance with my duty as I see it.

House of Commons, February 24, 1942

Amid a restructuring of the War Cabinet, Churchill pledged to continue in his quest to victory with this commitment to duty.

We shall go forward together. The road upward is stony. There are upon our journey dark and dangerous valleys through which we have to make and fight our way. But it is sure and certain that if we persevere—and we shall persevere—we shall come through these dark and dangerous valleys into a sunlight broader and more genial and more lasting than mankind has ever known.

Leeds, May 16, 1942

During the thirty-third month of the war, he thanked the people of Leeds for their dedication to liberty and determination to serve the war effort.

Churchill ON COURAGE

*W*e must all drive ourselves to the utmost limit of our strength. We must preserve and refine our sense of proportion. We must strive to combine the virtues of wisdom and of daring. We must move forward together, united and inexorable.

Edinburgh, October 12, 1942

Churchill reminded the people of Edinburgh of the unbreakable spirit of Scottish warriors.

Among the qualities for which Scotland is renowned, steadfastness holds perhaps the highest place.

Edinburgh, October 12, 1942

He also reminded them of their great trek to meet the challenge of victory.

Churchill ON COURAGE

*W*e shall not fail, and then someday when children ask, "What did you do to win this inheritance for us, and to make our name so respected among men?", one will say: "I was a fighter pilot"; another will say: "I was in the Submarine Service"; another: "I marched with the Eighth Army"; a fourth will say: "None of you could have lived without the convoys of the Merchant Seamen"; and you in your turn will say, with equal pride and with equal right: "We cut the coal."

Coal Owners and Miners Conference, Central Hall, Westminster, October 31, 1942

The coal industry was the first industry Churchill addressed as an industry during the war, declaring, "War is made with steel, and steel is made with coal." He knew the miners may have felt left out of the national war effort, so he reminded them that their work formed the very spine of that effort. His words remind us to honor the contributions of each team member.

Churchill ON COURAGE

You must never make a promise which you do not fulfil.

House of Commons, November 11, 1942

Sharing a war analysis, he cited pledges to Russia to draw German fire along the French coast and in the Middle East.

Churchill ON COURAGE

I am certainly not one of those who need to be prodded. In fact, if anything, I am a prod.

House of Commons, November 11, 1942

Churchill boasted of his insatiable call to duty and his belief in the process of initiative.

The problems of victory are more agreeable than those of defeat, but they are no less difficult.

House of Commons, November 11, 1942

With Allied success in North Africa, Churchill shared the belief that managing victories would pose countless challenges. He encouraged all to summon the spirit of victory to enhance the overall quality of the war effort. This speech also began to condition Britain to recognize and accept the challenges of eventual peacetime adjustment.

Churchill ON COURAGE

*W*e must not build on hopes or fears, but only on the continued faithful discharge of our duty, wherein alone will be found safety and peace of mind.

World Broadcast, London, November 29, 1942

Churchill warned that victory was not certain, and the ordeal of war could be long.

*L*et us go forward together and put the great principles we support to the proof.

Bradford, December 5, 1942

The great cause, as Churchill saw it, was "freedom and justice . . . the weak against the strong, law versus violence, and mercy and tolerance versus brutality and iron-bound tyranny."

Churchill ON COURAGE

We desire only to be judged by results.

House of Commons, February 11, 1943

U-boat sinkings were increasing. Rommel was retreating in North Africa. The British had freed Tripoli. Churchill urged the public to support the war effort and create victory.

Churchill ON COURAGE

*L*eft to itself, opportunity may easily lead to divergency.

House of Commons, June 8, 1943

Citing the shift to an offensive war phase, Churchill insisted that greater communication between allies was essential to best plan the war effort.

*T*yranny is our foe, whatever trappings or disguise it wears, whatever language it speaks, be it external or internal, we must forever be on our guard, ever mobilized, ever vigilant, always ready to spring at its throat.

Harvard University, Cambridge, September 6, 1943

Churchill encouraged the audience to reject and obliterate the evil of tyranny.

*Y*ou have to run risks. There are no certainties in war. There is a precipice on either side of you—a precipice of caution and a precipice of over-daring.

House of Commons, September 21, 1943

The Allies invaded Italy, facing stubborn German resistance. Churchill called for the troops to face the challenge with passion and determination.

Churchill ON COURAGE

I have no fear of the future. Let us go forward into its mysteries, let us tear aside the veils which hide it from our eyes, and let us move onward with confidence and courage.

London, September 28, 1943

Speaking to six thousand women in Albert Hall, the sixty-eight-year-old Prime Minister praised women's roles "in our struggle for right and freedom."

Churchill ON COURAGE

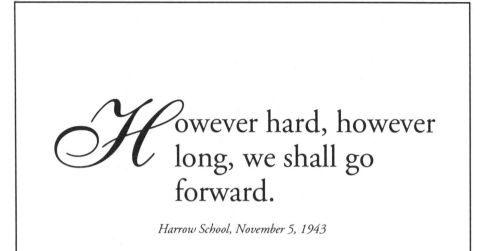

However hard, however long, we shall go forward.

Harrow School, November 5, 1943

At his beloved school he explained the "path of war is hard and long and the end uncertain, but essential."

Churchill ON COURAGE

The penalties of defeat are frightful.

House of Commons, February 22, 1944

Churchill warned all to recognize the hazards of defeat.

*T*his is no time for sorrow or rejoicing. It is a time for preparation, effort, and resolve.

House of Commons, February 22, 1944

Churchill called for Britain to focus its attention and will to the task of victory.

Churchill ON COURAGE

*I*t is to this task that we must vow ourselves everyday anew. It is to this ordeal that we must address our minds with all the moral fortitude we possess. The task is heavy, the toil is long, and the trials will be severe. Let us all try our best to do our duty. Victory may not be far away, and will certainly not be denied us in the end.

House of Commons, February 22, 1944

Churchill offered assurances while demanding perseverance.

*T*he longer you can look back, the farther you can look forward.

The Royal College of Physicians, London, March 2, 1944

Citing the four hundred-year-old college's traditions, he observed, "The wider the span, the longer the continuity, the greater is the sense of duty in individual men and women, each contributing their brief life's work to the preservation and progress of the land in which they live, the society of which they are members, and the world of which they are members."

Churchill ON COURAGE

*N*o reasonable person
could expect us to solve
all the problems of the world
while we are fighting for our lives.

House of Commons, April 21, 1944

Amid debate and constant criticism, Churchill
reminded his critics of their most essential duty and
the fact that all in such complex and challenging
times cannot be managed perfectly.

Churchill ON COURAGE

*W*hen the signal came, from the poorest Colony to the most powerful Dominion, the great maxim held: "When the King declares war, the Empire is at war." The darkest moment came. Did anyone flinch? Was there one cry of pain or doubt or terror? No, sir, darkness was turned into light, and into a light which will never fade away.

House of Commons, April 21, 1944

In this remarkable statement, Churchill summarized the aftermath of World War I and the ready justice—accepted immediately by every British subject—of entering World War II against the Nazi storm.

Churchill ON COURAGE

*W*hat is this force, this miracle which makes governments, as proud and sovereign as any that have ever existed, immediately cast aside all their fears, and immediately set themselves to aid a good cause and beat the common foe? You must look very deep into the heart of man, and then you will not find the answer unless you look with the eye of the spirit. Then it is that you learn that human beings are not dominated by material things, but by ideas for which they are willing to give their lives or their life's work.

House of Commons, April 21, 1944

Churchill praised all whose full and complete response was to do their duty to support "freedom, liberty, hope, goodness."

*W*e must respect the rights and opinions of others, while holding firmly to our own faith and convictions.

House of Commons, May 24, 1944

After reviewing the world situation, Churchill called for a world of peace formed by differing, yet united, nations.

Churchill ON COURAGE

*L*et us go on then to battle on every front . . . Bear with unflinching fortitude whatever evils and blows we may receive. Drive on through the storm, now that it reaches its fury, with the same singleness of purpose and inflexibility of resolve as we showed to the world when we were all alone.

House of Commons, August 2, 1944

Citing the Allies' success at Normandy, the safe relocation of one million civilians from London, British tank superiority, and exceptional war planning, he continued to urge total commitment to victory.

Churchill ON COURAGE

I am sure this is no time for taking hard and fast momentous decisions on incomplete data and at breakneck speed. Hasty work and premature decisions may lead to penalties out of all proportion to the issues immediately involved.

House of Commons, September 28, 1944

At sixty-nine, he encouraged all to patiently consider the war's concluding months and decisions and the delicacy of managing its aftermath.

Churchill ON COURAGE

*I*t is always in the last lap that races are either gained or lost. The effort must be forthcoming. This is no moment to slacken.

London, November 9, 1944

Rome, Athens, Paris, Brussels, and Belgrade had been liberated, and the U-boat menace had been quelled, yet German resistance would be fierce.

*I*t is a mistake to look too far ahead. Only one link in the chain of destiny can be handled at a time.

House of Commons speech after the Yalta Conference, February 27, 1945

Churchill carefully reviewed what he saw as an evolving "new world structure" of friendly diplomacy and cautious optimism.

Churchill ON COURAGE

God bless you all. This is your victory!

V-E Day Speech to the British, London, May 8, 1945

Following the unconditional surrender of German forces, Churchill praised and thanked all in Britain who stood the test for freedom. "Everyone," he said, "man or woman, has done their best."

Churchill ON COURAGE

*L*et us then march steadily along that plain and simple line.

House of Commons, August 16, 1945

Churchill was defeated by the Labour Party soon after V-E Day in June. Following the Japanese surrender in August, he cited the need to reconstruct nations "torn and convulsed by war," warning that democracy would be on trial.

We must try to share blessings and not miseries.

House of Commons, August 16, 1945

Urging all to celebrate hope and cherish and share good fortune, he called for the rapid return and reunification of service personnel with their families.

Churchill ON COURAGE

Greatheart must have his sword and armour to guard the pilgrims on their way.

Richmond, Virginia, March 8, 1946

Accompanied by General Dwight Eisenhower, Churchill praised the Virginia General Assembly as "guardians of this sacred flame" of liberty while encouraging all to be vigilant and prepared.

*T*he changes which are unavoidable from time to time as the spirit of humanity develops, either forwards, or sometimes in another direction, can be solved in free debate.

Norwegian Parliament, Oslo, Norway, May 13, 1948

Churchill encouraged respect for the process of parliamentary debate.

There was also that constant repetition, time after time, of desperate adventures which marked the work of the Commandos, as of the submarines, requiring not only hearts of fire but nerves of tempered steel.

The Commando Memorial unveiling, Westminster Abbey, London, May 21, 1948

Here he praised the spirit of courageous determination so often exhibited by British commandos.

Churchill ON COURAGE

*T*o perceive a path and to point it out is one thing, but to blaze the trail and labour to construct the path is a harder task.

House of Commons, May 12, 1949

Churchill applauded the negotiation of the Atlantic Pact with the United States.

Churchill ON COURAGE

*A*t this moment everyone ought to consider very carefully what is his duty towards his country, towards the causes he believes in, towards his home and family, and to his own personal rights and responsibilities.

Political Broadcast, January 21, 1950

At seventy-five, Churchill reentered the political fray to unseat the Socialist government. He called for his countrymen to clarify and follow their most strategic values.

Churchill ON COURAGE

*C*lass quarrels, endless party strife, on a background of apathy, indifference, and bewilderment, will lead us all to ruin. Only a new surge of impulse can win us back the glorious ascendancy which we gained in the struggle for right and freedom, and for which our forbears had nerved our hearts down the long aisles of time. Let us make a supreme effort to surmount our dangers. Let faith, not appetite, guide our steps.

Political Broadcast, January 21, 1950

Churchill urged all to reconcile hope and belief to create a nation of revival and glory.

*T*o maintain a robust and lively progress, all adventurous and enterprising spirits should have their chance to try, and, if they fail, to try again.

Leeds, February 4, 1950

Churchill decried the burdens of Socialist taxation, which he saw as an obstacle to the creation of new business ventures.

Churchill ON COURAGE

Above all things we must make sure that our foundations are not undermined.

Election Address, Leeds, February 4, 1950

He called for voters to rise to the challenge to reestablish Britain's might among nations and in the eyes of the British.

Churchill ON COURAGE

*I*f ever there was a moment, when, after all our victories and service to the cause of human freedom, every patriotic man and woman ought to be thinking about the country and taking a long view, that moment is now.

Election Address, Leeds, February 4, 1950

Churchill urged all to work to "save ourselves in peace."

Churchill ON COURAGE

*I*n our view the strong
should help the weak.

Election Address, Devonport, February 9, 1950

He decried the Socialists' view that "the strong
should be kept down to the level of the weak in order
to have equal shares for all."

Churchill ON COURAGE

*A*t least I feel that Christian men should not close the door upon any hope of finding a new foundation for the life of the self-tormented human race. What prizes lie before us; peace, food, happiness, leisure, wealth for the masses never known or dreamed of; the glorious advance into a period of rest and safety for all the hundreds of millions of homes where little children play by the fire and girls grow up in all their beauty and young men march to fruitful labour in all their strength and valour. Let us not shut out the hope that the burden of fear and want may be lifted for a glorious era from the bruised and weary shoulders of mankind.

Election Address, Edinburgh, February 14, 1950

While sharply criticizing Prime Minister Attlee's Socialist goals, Churchill called for a restoration of hope.

Churchill ON COURAGE

*Y*ou must not blind yourselves to the fact that many grievous difficulties lie ahead.

Political Broadcast, London, February 17, 1950

Churchill called for all to be wary of the coming devaluation under the nation's Socialist leadership, and to study and weather the storm.

Churchill ON COURAGE

*B*ut while God gives me
the strength, and the
people show me their good will,
it is my duty to try, and try I will.

Political Broadcast, London, February 17, 1950

At seventy-five, Churchill reminded his constituents
of his absolute dedication to duty in his quest to again
lead his troubled land.

Churchill ON COURAGE

I could be well content that others should bear the burden, but while I have life and strength I feel it my duty not to desert the fighting line, and I come before you now to ask you to stand by me giving me the best backing you can.

Election Address, Loughton, February 18, 1950

Citing the threat of major economic crisis, he called for voters to allow him to lead Britain out of what he termed a "temporary eclipse."

Churchill ON COURAGE

*T*he dominant forces in human history have come from the perception of great truths and the faithful persuance of great causes.

House of Commons, March 28, 1950

Churchill praised the concepts of inspiration and duty when establishing international agreements.

Churchill ON COURAGE

*E*veryone has his day and some days last longer than others.

House of Commons, January 30, 1952

Discussing international policy, he observed that each day offers a season of change and choices.

Churchill ON COURAGE

*L*et us be united, and let our hopes lie in our unity.

The White House, Washington, D.C., May 6, 1959

Churchill called for greater unity and cooperation between Britain and the United States.

Churchill ON COURAGE

*L*et governments do what they will, our future rests on one foundation and one only—the courage, skill, enterprise, and ingenuity of our people. But we need more than just our native wit and intelligence. We need trained minds.

Woodford, September 29, 1959

Churchill saw education as a fundamental element of a courageous people.

The way ahead is a broad and clear one.

Woodford, October 31, 1959

At eight-four, he praised the political unity and dedication to the future evident at this time in Britain.

Churchill ON COURAGE

*B*y our courage, our endurance, and our brains we have made our way in the world to the lasting benefit of mankind. Let us not lose heart. Our future is one of high hope.

Woodford, October 31, 1959

At Woodford, Churchill again proclaimed his belief in a hope-filled future.

Churchill ON COURAGE

*O*ur past is the key to our future, which I firmly trust and believe will be no less fertile and glorious. Let no man underrate our energies, our potentialities, and our abiding power for good.

The Award of Honorary U.S. Citizenship, The White House, April 9, 1963

In his final speech, Churchill hailed the magnificent power of goodness.

Churchill ON COURAGE